Bats

Elizabeth Russell-Arnot

Contents

What are bats?	2
What bats look like	3
Bats' wings	4
Different bats eat different things	6
Bats in winter	8
Flying by ear	9
Bat homes	10
Bat babies	12
Friends and enemies	14
Bats get eaten too!	15
Where bats live	16
Index	17

What are bats?

Bats are **nocturnal** animals. This means that they sleep during the day and are awake at night.

What bats look like

Bats are the only mammals that can fly.

Bats have five toes on each of their very small feet.

Their bodies are covered with fur, which is usually dull brown or grey.

All bats have ears.

Most bats have small eyes, but fruit bats have large eyes.

Some bats have tails.
Most bats rest by hanging upside down.

What does nocturnal mean?

Bats' wings

The wings of bats
look like hands with long fingers.
Thin, soft, stretchy skin
joins their long fingers together.
This skin also joins the fingers
to the bats' back legs and tails.

Nocturnal means being awake at night and asleep during the day.

When a bat stretches out
its legs and fingers,
the skin makes wings,
and the bat can fly.

When their wings are folded up,
some bats can also
scurry around on the ground.

Can some bats move around on the ground?

Different bats eat different things

Some bats only eat insects.

Fruit bats eat fruit and drink the nectar of flowers. Their favourite fruits are mangoes and bananas.

Other bats eat both insects and fruit.

Yes. Some bats can move around on the ground when their wings are folded up.

Another type of bat eats fish.
It grabs them out of the water
with its large curved claws.

Bloodsucking bats, called **vampire bats**,
only drink animal blood.
Vampire bats have very sharp teeth
that they use to bite their victims.
Then they lick up the blood
with their tongues.

What do vampire bats feed on?

Bats in winter

Some bats eat a lot in autumn
and grow fat before winter comes.

In the winter,
the days and nights are cold
and there is very little food around.
Some bats fall into
a very deep sleep
until spring.
This is called **hibernation**.

Other sorts of bats fly away
to warmer places during winter.
This is called **migration**.

Vampire bats feed on animal blood.

Flying by ear

Most bats fly about at night,
so they need to have good hearing
to help them find their way in the dark.

While they are flying,
these nocturnal bats
make high-pitched sounds or squeaks
that people can't hear.

The squeaks bounce back (or echo)
from walls and trees,
and from flying insects.
The bats hear these echoes
and know what is around them,
and where their food is.

What does hibernate mean?

Bat homes

Most bats like to live together and sleep in dark places such as hollow trees and caves, or inside the roofs of buildings.

Thousands of bats sometimes sleep in the same cave.

Most bats sleep upside down, hanging on with their feet.

Some fruit bats sleep hanging in trees.

Hibernate means going to sleep for the winter.

Some female bats find a special cave,
called a **maternity cave**,
where they go to have their babies.
Nearly all of the babies are born
on the same day.

Male bats are not allowed
into the maternity cave.
They have to find
another place to sleep!

Where do bats like to sleep?

Bat babies

Most bats have one baby at a time. When it is born, it is blind and has no fur.

The baby bats drink milk from teats which are under their mothers' armpits.

When baby bats are feeding, they hang onto their mothers with their claws.

Bats like to sleep in dark places such as caves, hollow trees or under roofs.

While the mother bats are flying,
the baby bats also
hold onto a special teat
so they can stay close to their mothers.

When the baby bats become too heavy,
the mother bats leave their babies
behind when they go hunting.

Some bats can look after themselves
when they are only a few months old;
fruit bats are not completely grown-up
until they are twelve months old.

How many babies do bats have?

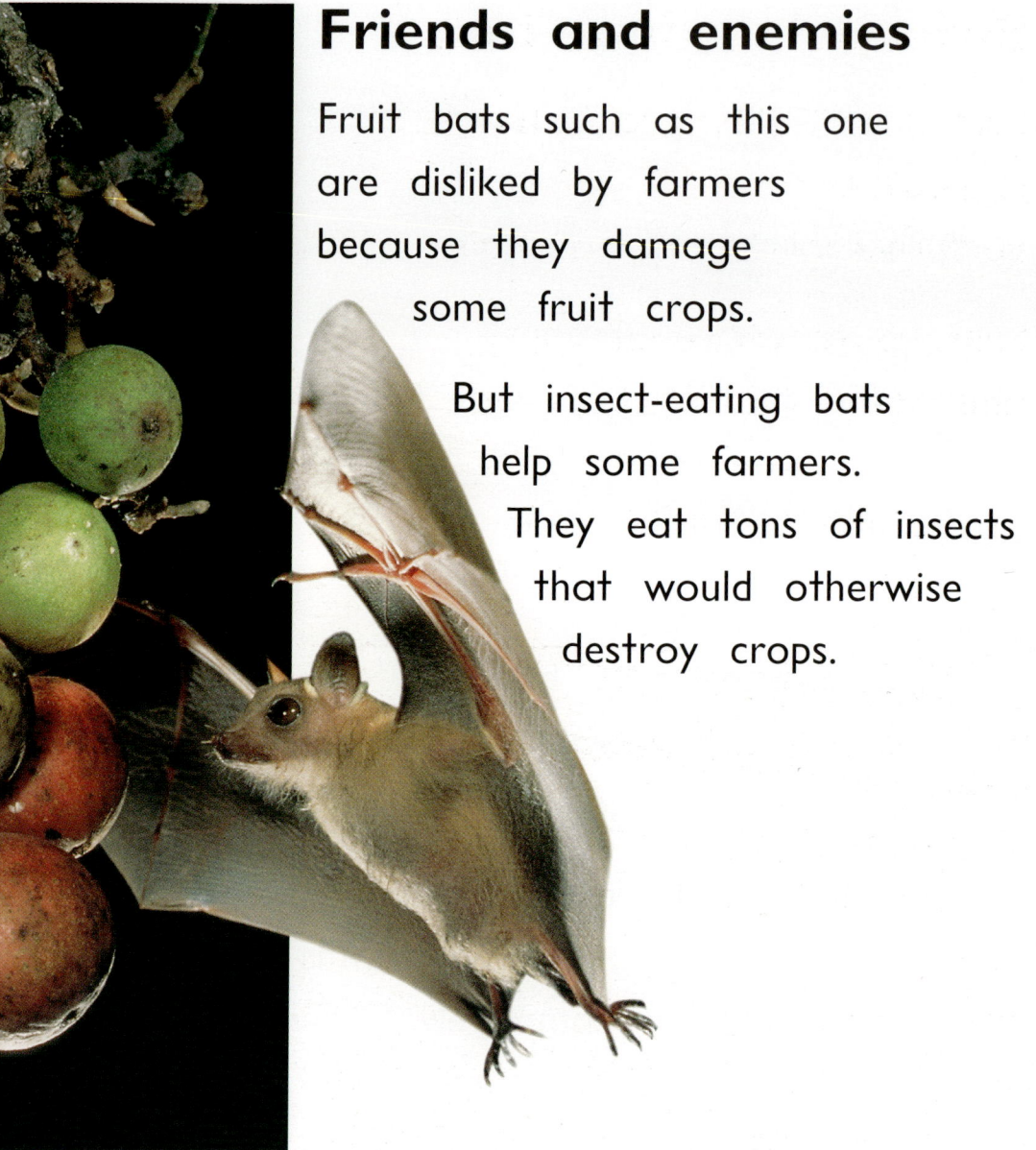

Friends and enemies

Fruit bats such as this one are disliked by farmers because they damage some fruit crops.

But insect-eating bats help some farmers. They eat tons of insects that would otherwise destroy crops.

Bats usually have only one baby at a time.

Bats get eaten, too!

Sometimes, bats are eaten by crocodiles, snakes, nocturnal birds or mammals.

Some bats will even kill and eat each other!

Are bats helpful to farmers?

Where bats live

Insect-eating bats are helpful to some farmers, but fruit bats can cause damage to crops.